One Classroom, Many Cultures

By Elizabeth Massie

Illustrated by Jill Dubin

Illustrated by Jill Dubin

ISBN-13: 978-0-328-83277-4
ISBN-10:　　0-328-83277-4
11　　20

Peek inside a store. Take a look at a park. Watch busy sidewalks. You will see many different people shopping, playing, and going places. Some are tall and others are short. Some have curly hair and others have straight hair. Some are young. Others are old.

The United States is a nation of many people. Some of them may have families that have lived here for hundreds of years. Some of them may have families that moved here from other countries not long ago. These people live in the same neighborhoods. The parents work together. The children go to school together.

Let's meet the students in Mr. Tucker's first-grade class. They have things in common. They study reading. They study math. They paint pictures and play games. Many of them are the same age. When something funny happens, they laugh!

The students are also different
in some ways. Some have blond hair.
Others have black or red hair.
Some are tall. Others are short.
Their families have come from different
places with different cultures.
Let's meet six of them.

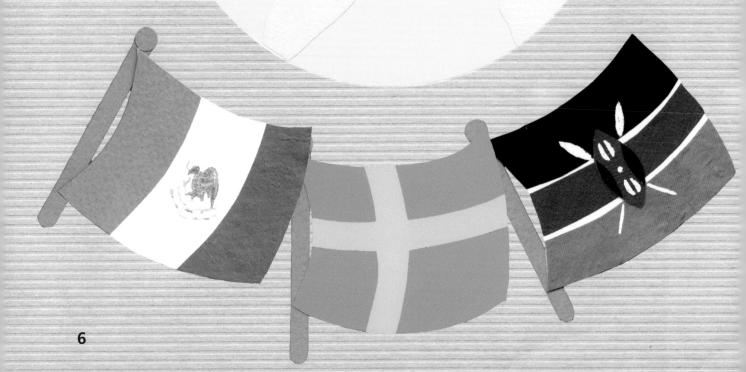

This is **Ama.**

Her family is Cherokee. The Cherokees are Native Americans. They have lived on the land that is the United States since before European settlers came.

Ama is a Cherokee name. It means "water." Ama loves to swim, so it is a good name for her!

Ama's parents often prepare traditional Cherokee foods. These include onions, eggs, watercress, crawdads, fry bread, and hominy. Hominy is a food made from corn kernels.

Ama's mother is a potter. She makes beautiful pots and bowls with Cherokee designs. She is teaching Ama how to make pots and bowls too.

Ama's family takes part in the Cherokee National Holiday. It is held once a year. Cherokee people from all over the country go to Oklahoma. They play traditional games such as Cherokee marbles. They share Cherokee foods. Ama's mother sells her bowls and pots.

This is Raul.

His family came to the United States from Mexico. In Raul's home, the family speaks both English and Spanish. Their house is their *casa*. Raul has a pet dog, or *perro*. Raul thinks it is cool to know two languages.

Some of Raul's favorite foods are Mexican.
His mother makes corn tortillas by hand. Raul
and his father fill the tortillas with black beans,
cheese, and beef for a tasty meal.

Raul's family celebrates Mexican Independence Day. On September 16, 1810, Mexicans began their fight for freedom from Spain. Now, on September 16, Raul's family takes part in a fiesta with others from Mexico. There is dancing, music, and fireworks. It is a happy time.

This is **Britta**.

Her family came to the United States from Sweden.

Britta's family likes foods from many cultures. Britta loves pizza best! However, once a week Britta's parents fix a traditional Swedish meal. They have smoked salmon or meatballs with potatoes. But they always have bread pudding for dessert.

Britta's name means "strong." She loves to dance. When she dances she feels happy and strong. She enjoys Swedish polska (POLE-skah) music. This music is fast and lively. It is usually played on a fiddle.

People in Sweden have a celebration in June. It is called Midsummer. Britta's great-grandmother used to live in Sweden. She remembers gathering flowers to wear in her hair for Midsummer. She remembers dancing around a pole and eating strawberries. Now, she fixes flowers for Britta's hair each June to remember Midsummer. The family eats fresh summer strawberries.

This is **Joseph**.

He and his brother Charles came to the United States from Kenya. Joseph was only three years old then. They live with Joseph's aunt and uncle.

Joseph's aunt serves Kenyan foods. One of Joseph's favorites is fish stew. He also likes coconut rice. The family follows Kenyan customs at dinnertime. The family eats with their right hands only. Fruits, not sweets, are served for dessert.

Joseph loves to run. Many of the world's fastest marathon runners come from Kenya. Joseph races Charles around the park several times. They are so fast they look like blurs passing by!

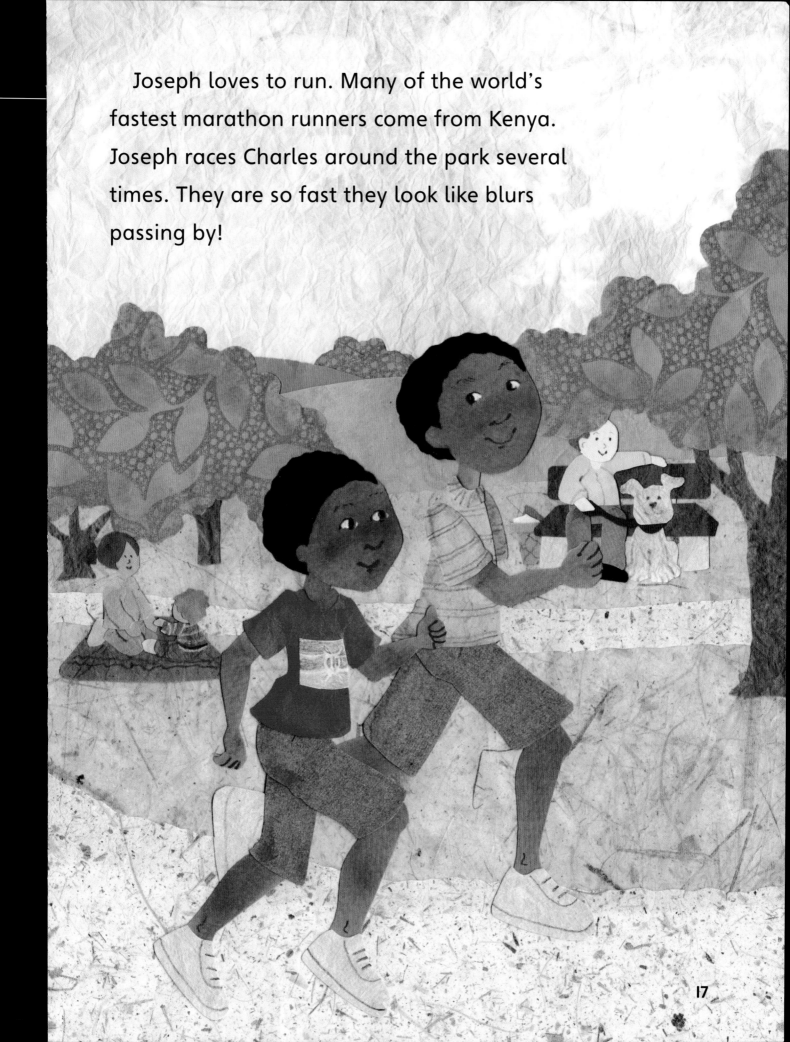

Joseph's uncle plays a Kenyan drum. It is made of hollow wood covered in cowhide. Sometimes at night the family gets together to dance while Joseph's uncle plays. It reminds them of their homeland. Joseph misses Kenya sometimes. Still, he is happy to be in the United States.

This is Miyu.

Her family came to the United States from Japan.

Miyu's family follows some Japanese traditions at home. They take off their shoes and put on slippers as they enter the house. Miyu's family members bow to one another to show respect. They sit on the floor at a low table when they eat.

Miyu and her family often dine on Japanese foods. Two of Miyu's favorites are shrimp and rice. The family serves food on several small dishes, not one big plate. The family uses chopsticks instead of forks.

They enjoy tea in the afternoon. The family often gathers to relax and sip tea together.

Miyu loves to draw and paint. Sometimes
she creates her own cartoon characters. Other
times she paints traditional pictures of bamboo,
waves, flowers, or mountains.

This is **Suhe**.

His family moved to the United States from Mongolia a year ago. He is still learning to speak English. His friends in the class help him.

Suhe had a horse when he lived in Mongolia. There were many horses there. Someday Suhe would like another horse. He is an excellent rider.

The family keeps many Mongolian traditions. Suhe does not walk in front of older people because it is considered rude. Suhe's family always holds the cups by the bottom when they have a drink. When they give or receive a gift, they make sure their sleeves are rolled down first.

Most of the time Suhe's family speaks Mongolian at home. If Suhe wants an apple, he will ask for an "ah-lim." If he wants potatoes, he will ask for "toe-mis."

Every student in Mr. Tucker's class has a family from a different culture. They share with each other. They learn from each other. Together, they make a wonderful class.